CREATIVE BOOT CAMP

An Interactive Journal of Eclectic Exercises to Jump-Start Your Creativity

By Nannette Stone

PETER PAUPER PRESS, INC.
WHITE PLAINS, NEW YORK

To the nine muses who inspire me and bring me joy:
Dayna, Tala, Danae, Joe, Ernie, Jack, Michael, Hugo, and Xavier—
in the order in which they appeared

PETER PAUPER PRESS
Fine Books and Gifts Since 1928

OUR COMPANY

In 1928, at the age of twenty-two, Peter Beilenson began printing books on a small press in the basement of his parents' home in Larchmont, New York. Peter—and later, his wife, Edna—sought to create fine books that sold at "prices even a pauper could afford."

Today, still family owned and operated, Peter Pauper Press continues to honor our founders' legacy—and our customers' expectations—of beauty, quality, and value.

Image on p. 78 © Nannette Stone
The Thinker image on page 58 and *Mona Lisa* image on pages 60-64 acquired from Wikimedia Commons.
All other images, graphics, and borders used under license from Shutterstock.com.

Visit us at www.peterpauper.com

When I say artist I don't mean in
the narrow sense of the word—

but the man who is building things—
creating molding the earth...

some with a brush—some with a shovel—
some choose a pen.

–JACKSON POLLOCK

Why should we use all our creative power....?
Because there is nothing that makes people so generous,
joyful, lively, bold and compassionate...

–BRENDA UELAND

Introduction

It's kind of fun to do the impossible.

–WALT DISNEY

WELCOME TO CREATIVE BOOT CAMP.

Creativity is above all a matter of attitude. It's a curious, focused, playful, and open-minded take on life. A habit of considering lots of alternatives before settling on a right solution. A willingness to experiment. Passion-driven activity and a desire to fully taste your own life.

You're an artist, and that's that.
When we're giving our best, we're being artistic.
When you're bringing your whole self to the party,
you're making poetry happen—
and you do it all the time, naturally.

–DANIELLE LAPORTE

You ARE creative. Artists and writers are creative. So are butchers, bakers, candlestick makers, social workers, business managers, math teachers, and security guards.

Your DNA has creativity stamped all over it. As sure as you were born with opposable thumbs, you have all the Darwinian advantages that your Stone Age ancestors used to capture fire and invent that first wheel. You arrived preprogrammed to pretend, improvise, and dance. You repurposed kitchen utensils into percussion instruments and enthusiastically experimented with gravity even before you outgrew your high chair. It's part of being human.

If you think all your flair got shelved with your toys and other childish things, you're underestimating yourself. The creativity you may doubt sustained you through every one of your largely unscripted days. You make plans and fantasize about what you love. And if you choose to, you can bump up that creative power to become more productive and to make life more fun.

If you've already developed your creative bent, you can super-size it and kick it into orbit. As you will learn in this manifesto to *your* creativity, it's a matter of psychology, tried-and-true methodology, a little magic, and neuroscientific fact.

If you are curious and willing to try new things, and are ready to put in the effort, then all you need is know-how and desire. Many theorists believe that your level of motivation is the single most important determinant of your creative ability.

So in short, if you want more creative muscle and are willing to do the work—it's all yours.

Hide not your Talents, they for Use were made. What's a Sun-Dial in the Shade!

–BENJAMIN FRANKLIN

YOUR HELP WANTED

PARTNERSHIP POSITION AT MUSES UNLIMITED
NO EXPERIENCE NECESSARY

**Do you long for a bigger, more productive life?
Do you want to turn your work into play
and your play into work?**

THEN WE WANT YOU!

With our epic record of genius and your unique personal qualities we can make beautiful music together. Or novels, scientific discoveries, fashion, plays, cartoons...

WHATEVER YOUR HEART TELLS YOU TO DO

Just show up for work on a consistent basis, dare to think new thoughts, and participate in novel activities. If you are willing to keep a notebook or voice recorder and/or a small digital camera handy, and agree to listen to our direction whenever and wherever you are—

then don't call us.

WE ARE ALREADY CALLING YOU!

Rules and Tools

Creativity is often about breaking old rules. You don't have to complete this book in order, or in any particular way at all. Write a little or a lot. Take prompts seriously or don't. Skip around. Dig deep. Crack jokes.

The following things, however, will help you get the most out of your *Creative Boot Camp* journey.

1. **Be prepared!** Train your mind's eye to be ever alert to beauty, humor, interesting questions, gifts of inspiration, and opportunities to learn and grow.

2. **Do morning pages** just as creativity guru Julia Cameron (*The Artist's Way*) advises. First thing each morning, write three pages in longhand. What you write doesn't need to be good or even consequential. You can complain, ramble, or repeat yourself over and over until the pages are filled. You don't have to go back and read them. They are for clearing your head. Recurring dreams and complaints may point you in a new direction. Your text is likely to be raw, but if you feel up to it, go through with a highlighter at a later date to salvage the occasional bright thought or great turn of phrase.

3. **Keep your smartphone, a recording device or camera, or a small notebook** nearby so that your good ideas don't sneak away from you. Pick up a waterproof notepad if your muse likes to drop in while you shower.

4. **Keep a journal.** Size matters. You'll want to have a small notebook to jot down your thoughts during the day, but your journal should give your imagination room to stretch out. If you want to expand on the exercises you start in this book (as you hopefully will), go to your journal. A binder will do, but if you're a visual thinker, consider pasting your scribbles, sketches, and photos onto the pages of a large discarded book where you can embellish them later with paint, scraps of paper, and pictures that represent your creative goals.

5. Optional gear is an **"idea piggy bank"**: a box or trunk to store larger objects and artifacts that can enliven memories through scent and feel. Maps, menus, theater programs, an old report card, vials of perfume, a garment, a souvenir, an expired passport can sometimes trigger a work rich with detail.

Yes, If...?

Indomitable imagineer Walt Disney insisted his employees embrace the same "Yes, if" approach that he used to turn a mouse into a movie star, and his nest into the Magic Kingdom. A "No, because..." stance can wither budding thoughts or ideas while still on the vine. But a "Yes, if..." line of thinking can nudge your creativity up a rung and turn more of your possibilities into plausibilities.

"Yes, if...?" can be used like a game. Challenge a kid or an adult with an inventive mind to answer progressively outrageous suggestions in clever ways to make them hypothetically feasible. It's a way to stretch the imagination, and practice suspending judgment long enough to see the great idea hidden within a ridiculous one.

Or "Yes, if...?" can be a way to pry more results from the questions you ask yourself.

Stay in the yes zone and try one.

Why not .... **?**

(your idea or dream)

Yes, if .... **!**

(What conditions need to be met and how could it be done?)

Adding "Yes, if?" attitude to your arsenal of creative tools makes everything easier. It's a weapon of mass construction. Who knows what long shots you'll be able to turn into sure things?

■ Drum up a few "Yes, if…" plausibilities.

Why not

Yes, if

Kick-Start Your Creative Genius

Every now and then a man's mind is stretched by a new idea or sensation, and never shrinks back to its former dimensions.
–OLIVER WENDELL HOLMES, SR.

You can trip the switch that makes your brain generate more possibilities in a matter of moments and with no more effort than it takes to make a sandwich. Dr. Simone Ritter, of Radboud University Nijmegen, has conducted studies showing that active participation in any novel experience instantly ramps up creativity. Students who spent a few minutes getting disoriented in a virtual reality environment immediately improved their scores on creativity tests that involved generating novel answers to open-ended questions. But so did students who were just asked to change the way they prepared their standard Dutch breakfast (chocolate sprinkles on bread).

Making your morning meal upside down will not turn you into a creative genius overnight, but it might disrupt something called "functional fixedness"—the tendency to perceive things only in terms of their original intended purpose. Functional fixedness is a major roadblock to creative problem-solving and inspired re-envisioning. Counteract it and who knows what you'll come up with.

The suggestions sprinkled throughout this book are meant to jump-start your ideas about how to do just that. Try not to skip exercises just because they feel odd or because you don't see an immediate relevance to your goals. A peculiar fit can be a beneficial fit if it makes you stretch your behavioral repertoire. Choose the activities that deviate most from your norm to maximize your "aha!" moments. But stay near the margins of your comfort zone. Go for exciting and a little awkward, not terrifying or embarrassing. Do use your imagination to repeat, modify, or reinvent prompts (creatively) as you wish.

■ What routines could you disrupt? Change the hand you use to brush your teeth? Pick a different route to work? Revamp the way or order in which you do a household task?

....

....

....

....

■ Choose one routine and devise several surprising ways you could switch it up.

....

....

....

....

....

Be a Thrill Seeker

To perk up your brain and increase its neural pathways, do something new and thrilling. You get to have a blast while your ability to generate new ideas gets a leg up.

■ Is there something you once enjoyed but haven't done for so long it's new again? (Could you reclaim the pleasure of gliding down the street on inline skates? Coasting downhill on a sled or a bike? Riding a horse? Driving your car with all the windows rolled down to feel the wind?)

■ Shoot some hoops if you've never dribbled a basketball. Take a tap dancing class, especially if you're the type who doesn't even slow dance. What out-of-your-norm activity are you ready to try?

....

....

....

....

....

■ What are some out-of-this-world challenges you might enjoy? Scuba dive to know weightlessness? Climb an observation tower to feel closer to the sky? Float above the world in a hot air balloon?

....

....

....

....

....

....

■ Finally, what unique and enlivening sensations can you discover right at home? Twirling or dancing around the house while you pick up clutter (or not)? Running through a lawn sprinkler? Squeezing sand or mud between your toes?

....

....

....

....

....

....

....

....

....

....

....

....

We crave for new sensations but soon become indifferent to them.
The wonders of yesterday are today common occurrences.

—NIKOLA TESLA

The Crystal Ball Test

Put a dot anywhere on this page.

Now turn the page. ➞

Where you placed the dot does not by itself say much about your creative capacity. But how and why you made your choice might help you explore how you express it.

How did you choose where your dot would go?

....
....
....

If you just made a random mark, were you being dismissive, impatient, or playfully spontaneous? How do you usually respond to ambiguous situations?

....
....
....

Did you consider other alternatives?

....
....
....

Make more than one dot?

....
....
....

Did you try to figure out what might be the right or most creative answer? Does fear of being wrong or looking bad inhibit your creativity? If so, how?

....
....
....
....
....

How did your choice reflect your usual approach to open-ended problems?

....
....
....

What did you think on learning that there were no right answers?

....
....
....
....

Adapted from Edward de Bono.

Your Creative Style

■ When you create, are you usually methodical and meticulous? Or do you favor playful spontaneity and following your intuition?

....

....

....

....

....

....

■ If you favor one method over the other, are you open to the benefits of straying from your *modus operandi* on occasion? How so?

....

....

....

....

....

■ What do you do especially well?

....

....

....

....

....

....

■ When have you improvised? Come up with a last minute present, substituted a hairpin for a tool, given an impromptu toast at an affair?

....

....

....

....

....

....

■ What motivates you? (Is it the innate pleasure of doing the work? The opportunity to help others, convey a message, bring joy, raise questions, gain prestige, or monetary rewards? What else?)

....

....

....

....

....

....

■ When have you been able to initiate a conversation with someone very different from yourself? Put someone at ease? Defuse an uncomfortable social situation?

....

....

....

....

....

....

....

....

■ Do you have a good eye for proportion or color? Do you notice or make things that are interesting or beautiful? Do you draw, paint, take pictures, or decorate? Arrange food or hair? Elaborate here!

....

....

....

....

....

■ Do you play an instrument? Compose? Perform? Sing in the shower? Have you been able to pick out a tune on a piano or guitar? When everyone sings *Happy Birthday*, do you find yourself breaking out in harmony? Describe your musical proclivities.

....

....

....

....

....

....

....

■ Are you resourceful? Have you ever played refrigerator roundup (been short on groceries but pulled together a great meal using ingredients not usually served together)? How have you successfully used the tools at your disposal in an unconventional manner to achieve a goal?

....

....

....

....

....

....

■ Do you have survival creativity? How have you been able to make do, avoid danger, or think on your feet in a dangerous situation?

....

....

....

....

....

....

....

■ Relationships thrive on thoughtful, imaginative touches. When are you able to be an active listener? Do you take note of what makes someone feel special and find ways to communicate that to them? If so, how?

....

....

....

....

....

....

■ Can you make a bad situation into an opportunity to learn? Describe a time when you were able to reframe the meaning of an event or someone's behavior in a way that invited understanding rather than irritation.

....

....

....

....

....

....

■ Can you tell a story about a mundane event in a riveting way? Do you write? Are you sensitive to the music of language? Are your texts and emails clever?

....

....

....

....

■ How have you altered something in a useful or enjoyable way? Cut up an item of clothing to give it a different slant? Shaped a tree into a bonsai? Changed the sound your doorbell makes?

....

....

....

....

■ Are you good at grasping the big picture? Can you determine what is important, and get right to the point? How so?

....

....

....

....

Psychologist Abraham Maslow called the knack for finding ways to sweeten life and make it run more smoothly "self-actualization." He pointed out that transforming an ordinary activity into something extraordinary is as much a creative accomplishment as fine painting or beautiful music.

■ What ordinary task or pastime do you approach creatively?

....

....

....

■ In what new directions might you take your interests and talents?

....

....

....

....

■ When can you start?

....

....

....

Never, never rest contented with any circle of ideas,
but always be certain that a wider one is still possible.
—RICHARD JEFFERIES

Your Creative History

There is a vitality, a life force, an energy, a quickening that is translated through you into action, and because there is only one of you in all of time, this expression is unique. And if you block it, it will never exist through any other medium and it will be lost.

—MARTHA GRAHAM

There is no one-size-fits-all kind of creativity because creativity is not an isolated trait.

Your "aha!" moments are unique because they incorporate everything about you—your life history, your personality, everything you know, and what you love. Your creativity is multifaceted and ever-evolving because *you* are.

■ Recall your earliest creative undertaking. How old were you? Were you encouraged?

....

....

....

....

....

■ What is the most recent creative thing you've done?

....

....

....

....

....

....

....

■ What is the best thing you've ever made or done?

....

....

....

....

....

....

....

■ When have you had a disappointing result?

....

....

....

....

....

■ What is your next idea?

....

....

....

....

....

■ When and under what circumstances have you most felt that you
were in the creative flow?

....

....

....

....

■ How much training do you have?

....

....

....

....

....

■ What and how much have you learned on your own?

....

....

....

....

....

■ Are your friends and family supportive of your endeavors?

....

....

....

....

....

How do you find inspiration?

Whose work do you admire, and why?

Creative Hindsight

An **egg of Columbus** is a creative idea, an answer to a puzzle, or a discovery that seems simple—even inevitable—only once it's been revealed. The name comes from an improbable story about Christopher Columbus. When detractors said that anyone could have made his famous voyage, he challenged them to stand an egg on its tip. When they failed, he tapped the egg on the table and flattened it just enough to balance it on end.

■ What egg of Columbus mysteries do you think you could have cracked? Are you incubating creative solutions to some puzzling issues right now?

....

....

■ When have you experienced enlightening breakthroughs, large or small, in any part of your life? Did they come from methodical analysis or arrive in a flash of insight?

....

....

....

....

A tangram is another kind of egg of Columbus—a puzzle in which you must assemble seemingly simple forms from a collection of odd shapes. Copy the egg below, and cut out its shapes, then try to reassemble them into the birds you see on the next page.

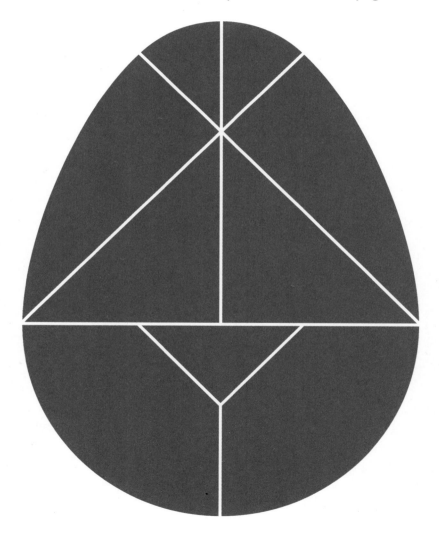

See the World Anew

Genius is no more than childhood recaptured at will, childhood equipped now with man's physical means to express itself, and with the analytical mind that enables it to bring order into the sum of experience.

—CHARLES BAUDELAIRE

One way to refresh your vision is to, literally, see the world through a child's eyes.

Spend some time giving your full attention to a young child (your own or one you've borrowed). Make it all about spontaneity, curiosity, and fun. Rediscover your "new" old world. Examine acorns and bugs with amazement. Imagine things, be superheroes, eat magic jelly sandwiches under a table, make up a story, invent a game.

Make your time with a child fun for both of you. If possible, don't spend too long staying still. It's a time to harvest vivid recollections of play. To experience childhood vicariously. Do any of these suggestions on the next page sound like fun to you?

Oh, the Thinks You Can Think!
—DR. SEUSS

■ Bring a ball of red string with you. Is it "spy string"? Stretched out between posts, trees, or chairs, does it turn into a laser beam that must be carefully crawled under and around? Did you bring it to play cat's cradle? See what else you and the child can think up to do with string.

■ Buy a roll of brown builder's paper from a hardware or craft store and trace life-sized body silhouettes onto it. Then, decorate the silhouettes with paint, markers, crayons, cut-up pictures from magazines, and anything else you can think of. There's plenty of paper on that roll. What else might you and your kid want to draw?

■ Use chalk to make a hopscotch pattern or something else on the driveway or sidewalk.

■ Remember discovering static electricity? Rub a balloon on wool and use it to make your hair stand on end. Or make a very thin slice of Styrofoam float like magic above your hands. What seemed like sorcery to you when you were little?

■ Bring a map for a nature walk or a treasure hunt. Visit a children's museum or a theme park. Ride a carousel. What are some activities a child makes you think of doing?

■ Don't forget about the cardboard box. It is so universally loved by children that it was inducted into the National Toy Hall of Fame in 2005.

■ As you play, encourage all those "why?" and "what if?" questions that strengthen thinking and creativity skills. Ask some of your own. Serious ones. Laughable ones. Be silly. Have a regular question lollapalooza.

■ End your visit with a grand finale. Will you light sparklers? Wish and blow on dandelions or toss coins into a water fountain?

Write about your experience on the next page.

It's never too late to have a happy childhood.
—TOM ROBBINS

■ What did you learn about play? About the child? About yourself?

Childhood Memories

"There's no use trying," said Alice. "One can't believe impossible things."

"I daresay you haven't had much practice," said the Queen. "When I was your age, I always did it for half-an-hour a day. Why, sometimes I've believed as many as six impossible things before breakfast."

— LEWIS CARROLL

What were you like as a kid?

....

....

What were your favorite activities?

....

....

What is the most fascinating childhood experience you can remember? How old were you?

....

....

When do you feel most playful and full of possibility now?

....

Melody of Language

As soon as I hear a sound, it always suggests a mood to me.
—BRIAN ENO

Notice the pure percussion and melody of language. Add unfamiliar and quaint words to your vocabulary for fun and to widen your fund of knowledge.

And when you are feeling **snerked** (gloomy) because your **darg** (day's work) has produced nothing but **old mung** (chicken mash), instead of treating yourself **felly** (harshly) you can just **deliciate** (indulge, make yourself happy) a little by playing with your new words.

■ Before you look them up, roll the following words over your tongue and set your imagination to work. What would happen in a story about one of these? What would they look like? Create a narrative, describe, draw, or collage.

poplolly?

....

....

widdershins?

....

....

snollygoster?

poop-noddy?

■ What musical instrument or melody is best suited for the…

whifling?

mumper?

■ What strange technique does a **faffling** use to hang from a tree branch?

■ It's no **hudder-mudder** (matter of secrecy) that archaic words are easy to find for free just by Googling. What others can you find?

Your Different Drummer

Move out of your comfort zone. You can only grow if you are willing to feel awkward and uncomfortable when you try something new.
–BRIAN TRACY

The instinct to follow the crowd is adaptive. Without it, collaboration and cooperation would be impossible. Man would never have survived, let alone developed a richly complex civilized society. But it can put a damper on individual expression.

It takes confidence to overcome the herd instinct (a.k.a. group think). In researcher Solomon Asch's famous 1951 experiment exploring conformity, 75 percent of those who took a "perceptual test" in a group setting gave very obviously incorrect answers after they heard everyone else in the room call them out. But if even one other person in that group answered correctly, only 5 to 10 percent of the subjects denied what they saw in order to fit in. Many people who went along with wrong answers said they did so to avoid ridicule, but a few actually decided the group must be right.

Can you buck the crowd? You don't have to be a maverick to be creative. Nevertheless, you'll be listening to your own drummer when you do your most exciting work.

■ **How strong is your instinct to go with the flow?**

....

....

....

■ **When has it served you well? When has it been counterproductive?**

....

....

....

■ **What kind of group think-induced biases lead to flawed decisions? What can be done to help elicit a healthier variety of questions and opinions in a group?**

....

....

....

....

Creative Brainstorming

Every revolutionary idea ... seems to evoke three stages of reaction.
They may be summed up by the phrases:

1 It's completely impossible.

2 It's possible, but it's not worth doing.

3 I said it was a good idea all along.

—ARTHUR C. CLARKE

*The mother of all brainstorming and problem-solving tools, **SCAMPER** is a mnemonic device created to help people remember to ask the questions that can lead to creative breakthroughs. Educator Bob Eberle originally developed it for children based on the ideas of writer Alex Osborn. Today, everyone from business professionals to songwriters uses it.*

Use the key words in as many ways as you can for an inexhaustible supply of new concepts.

First, review the central concepts and steps of the process. Then, on the pages that follow, workshop your own ideas. Select something you'd like to create or change—anything from a piece of music, a painting, or a business idea, to a scene from a play—and apply the SCAMPER method to transform it into something more interesting, beautiful, useful, or surprising.

SCAMPER:

SUBSTITUTE
COMBINE
ADAPT
MODIFY (or MAGNIFY)
PUT IT TO ANOTHER USE
ELIMINATE
REARRANGE (or REVERSE)

Scamper playfully through your field of interest on the next few pages to come up with fanciful and practical variations.

SUBSTITUTE

Replace part of the product or process. What person, place, thing, thought, or ingredient can be used instead?

Example: The substitution of artificial sweetener for sugar created diet soda.

Creative brainstorming: What if Beethoven's Fifth were performed on a harmonica or by a choir using kazoos instead of an orchestra? What if the people in your story were armadillos instead? (Would that be a cartoon?)

Your turn: Think of three hypothetical swaps you can make in your art, your thesis, your wardrobe, the way you use your space, or your business.

1 ....

....

....

2 ....

....

....

3 ....

....

COMBINE

Blend or bring together two or more unrelated materials in a new way. How can they be merged or collected in a way that makes the whole more interesting?

Example: Smartphones combine the functions of a phone, camera, music player, computer, calendar, and more.

Creative brainstorming: Could a vase hold an arrangement of lilies and origami? Could your novella be part graphic novel?

Your turn: Consider a number of combinations that could make something you do fresh. Could you bring together a diverse team of people to solve a problem in the community?

ADAPT

Borrow, emulate, and/or amend an existing idea or thing.

Example: The drive-through concept has been adapted by fast-food restaurants, banks, mailboxes, and pharmacies.

Creative brainstorming: Could an insulated food cooler be reconfigured into a pet carrier for better temperature control and soundproofing? Could a string hammock be hung as a window drape by day and a bed by night?

Your turn: Adaptation often leads to invention. Think of something you use often that could be better if tweaked in some way. Is there an item already on the market that could be used to improve something you make?

MODIFY (or MAGNIFY)

How can you switch up the shape, size, color, or texture? How can you expand, augment, or intensify?

Example: Aluminum construction in the 1970s allowed for over-sized heads on tennis rackets.

Creative brainstorming: Should it be smaller, concentrated, cut up, blurred? Funny instead of serious? Bigger? Rounder? Is something more interesting if bumpy, tiny, edible, or paper-thin? Fantasize the outlandish: a hologram dog that could entertain the children—no shedding, no accidents, no fleas.

Your turn: What three things would you want to look, feel, or work better in your art, business, or life? Imagine how you could alter each.

1

2

3

PUT IT TO ANOTHER USE

Can it be used for something else, or for more than one thing? Can it be repositioned or tapped in a new way?

Example: Recycled glass can become countertop composite.

Creative brainstorming: Imagine using pictures in frames as serving trays. What can be repurposed, and how?

Your turn: What would you like to see do double duty? Ignore practicalities in your beginning stages.

ELIMINATE

Streamline, simplify, or minimize.

Example: Classic examples are editing excess verbiage in writing or reducing clutter at home or work. In business, an example is removing preservatives and additives from a product to create a more natural food.

Creative brainstorming: Should you have fewer characters in your play? Cut a swath of trees to make a path through a wooded area? Take down a wall?

Your turn: What can you remove to make life simpler? Make room? Open up? Enhance a creation?

REARRANGE (or REVERSE)

Can parts of something be interchanged, inverted, or transposed? Can the sequence be switched up? Could you make a plan beginning with the desired outcome and design the steps leading up to it in reverse order?

Example: Fast-food restaurants instituted having customers pay for their meal before eating, reversing and streamlining the order.

Creative brainstorming: What if you place words in unusual patterns on a page? Apply paint to canvas, then sketch over it?

Your turn: Describe something in your life—from rearranging a room to making the ending of your screenplay the opening scene—that could benefit from this last call to action of SCAMPER.

....

....

....

....

....

....

....

....

There's nothing better than not knowing what's going to happen until you put the pieces together.

—FEIST

Intelligent Fast Failure

If he closes off every passageway and escape route, It's because he wants to show you a secret way which no one knows.
—RUMI

Did you fail at your last attempt to accomplish something? Good for you. (Imagine wild applause.) If you aren't failing at all in life, you probably aren't taking enough creative risks, and will never know how much you could have achieved.

The trick is to learn quickly from your failures and not get stuck. Dr. Jack Matson, a proud innovation junkie and a frequent failer, calls this process Intelligent Fast Failure or IFF.

In his creativity and innovation class for engineers, as in real life, serviceable right answers are not always the only or best ones. When challenged to build the highest possible tower out of 20 Popsicle sticks, those students who make the most failed attempts end up with the tallest structures. And it is contagious. In no time even the most initially conservative students catch on. Soon everyone starts having fun pushing the Popsicle tower envelope. Imagine split sticks, sticks stacked against walls and chairs.

IFFers are the movers and shakers of this world.

■ What flops, embarrassments, and incomplete endeavors in life slowed you down and which ones fortified your resolve?

....

....

....

....

■ What did you learn from them and how did you cope?

....

....

....

....

■ Does fear of failure prevent you from doing anything now? If so, how?

....

....

....

....

■ What is worth doing even if you don't succeed?

....
....
....
....

■ What's the worst thing that could happen if you goof up?

....
....
....
....

■ How would you manage or adapt? Who and what can you count on?

....
....
....
....
....

If only. Those must be the two saddest words in the world.
—MERCEDES LACKEY

Creativity Kleptomaniac

Imitation is not flattery. Transformation is flattery.
–AUSTIN KLEON

Take a page from Austin Kleon, author of the best-selling book, Steal Like an Artist. Be a creativity kleptomaniac. Eureka moments do not come out of a vacuum but rather from a shared culture. Sometimes genius is just a matter of revamping old work in inventive ways.

Even if you're not comfortable drawing, play with visual art. Trace photos, collage cut-out images, or use a lightbox. Norman Rockwell traced his own photographs and then used his artist's eye to exaggerate just the right details. There is even some evidence that early Renaissance painters used tracing and related techniques. As long as your work is transformational and not a copy, and you don't try to pass your work off as something it is not—enjoy!

Spatter this page with paint, Jackson Pollock-style. Or make some free-range dashes, dots, and squiggles with colored pencils and markers.

■ Put your own spin on Rodin's *The Thinker*. What's he pondering? Is he pausing for deep thought in the middle of a crowd? The middle of a lake? On the moon?

■ Repurpose a few words from a favorite song, saying, quotation, or poem. Alter the order and/or change the context to make them into comedic dialogue or a new verse.

....

....

....

....

....

....

■ Why stop there? Steal the best bits of conversation you overhear at a coffee shop, your neighbor's recipe for tiramisu, billboards, and bad puns! Try one here.

....

....

....

....

....

Dabble in more than one medium. Each thing you try will enhance your pleasure and inform your work in other areas.

The secret to creativity is knowing how to hide your sources.
—C.E.M. JOAD

Stealing Mona

The Mona Lisa *has been parodied more often than any other work of art. She's been an alligator, a vampire, a mosaic made of beer bottle caps, even a likeness rendered in staples. And she's still smiling! Doodle on her image. Go outside the lines and think of more interesting ways you could snatch her from da Vinci.*

■ Use her to design a billboard ad for a new brand—Renaissance Swimwear.

■ One theory is that Mona is a self portrait of the artist. Show her as a man.

■ Make her two years old.

■ Make her 80 years old. She can stand the test of time.

■ Transform her into something else. Can you see her as a puppet? A cake?

■ You find a letter written to her by da Vinci. What's in it?

....

....

....

....

....

....

....

■ You are Mona. Tell us: Is that a smirk? A smile? Indigestion?

....

....

....

....

....

....

....

....

Art Upside Down

Think you aren't creative because you can't draw?

Betty Edwards (*Drawing on the Right Side of the Brain*) demystified the art of drawing. She found that beginners draw better when they copy something that is upside down. It stops your logical brain from struggling to fill the page with a fixed notion of what it thinks things (an eye, an ear) should look like and helps you draw what you see instead. In her book she gave readers the task of copying Picasso's portrait of Igor Stravinsky upside down.

Whether you're a raw novice or an advanced draftsperson, give this exercise a shot. Copy the picture on the next page. Use a pencil with an eraser. Don't think about what you are drawing and don't try too hard. If you find it is difficult to calculate the distances between lines, cover the image and reveal small portions of it at a time as you draw. Keep at it. Try, try, again on several sheets of blank paper. Recognize the gems you produce along the way. Are they not two very creative camp boots?

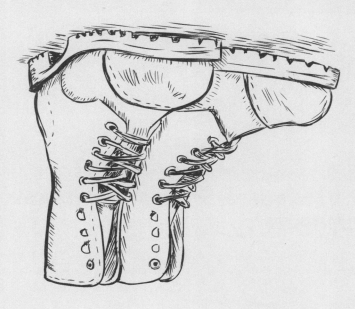

Humor

Words used carelessly, as if they did not matter in any serious way, often allowed otherwise well-guarded truths to seep through.

–DOUGLAS ADAMS

Humor is quintessential creativity. It toys with ideas. It challenges basic assumptions. It encourages spontaneity and fosters a solution-focused mindset.

Understand the basic blueprint for a joke and you have the formula for creativity.

A good joke sets up an expectation, builds suspense, and culminates in a twist that derails us and puts us back on course at the same time. The rush we feel when we get the joke is a sort of ha-ha-ha "aha."

Broaden your sense of humor to reinforce your creative mind and laugh it up to raise those creativity-enhancing endorphin levels. Read the funnies, clown around with friends, watch a comedy.

■ What makes you laugh out loud? Quick wit? Out-and-out slip-on-a-banana-peel slapstick? Puns? Practical jokes?

....

....

....

....

....

Take this joke! (Everyone else has.) Peter Sellers used it in *The Pink Panther Strikes Again*.

INSPECTOR CLOUSEAU: Does your dog bite?

HOTEL CLERK: No.

CLOUSEAU: Nice doggy! (He bends down to pet cute little dog. It snarls and bites him.) I thought you said your dog did not bite!

HOTEL CLERK: That is not my dog.

People who study comedy say that once stripped down, there are at most only seven jokes. Rewrite the "that's-not-my-dog" joke using your own details:

1. A thing or person who is being hurt or insulted in some way, and

2. A bystander, thought to be involved, who ignores or even encourages the act.

Try your hand at making these timeworn jokes new.

■ Why did the chicken (or anything else for that matter) cross the road?

....

....

....

....

■ A brunette, a redhead, and a blond walk into a bar...

....

....

....

....

....

■ What do you get when you cross a _____ with a _____?

....

....

....

....

....

Work Habits

Creativity is a habit, and the best creativity is the result of good work habits.

—TWYLA THARP

The verdict is in. Successful creative types, eccentric or not, are those who have highly organized, unyielding routines. The less wiggle room you give yourself about when and where to work, the more likely you are to follow through and meet your final goals. Do your work habits work for you?

A consistent time and a designated place to work might mean you hail a cab every morning at the same time (à la Twyla Tharp). Or you always write on the train (Alexander Chee's favorite). But any unbroken commitment to your work can work for you. It can be a predetermined number of hours, some measurable output, or even (if it's the best you can do) whenever and wherever you can shoehorn your craft between your parenting and your day job.

Complete the following pages to clarify your creative work habits.

How do you start your day?

....

....

....

What is your normal daily routine?

....

....

....

....

Describe the work habits you have now.

....

....

....

....

Do you schedule time to be creative?

....

....

....

■ How do you get into the creative zone?

....

....

....

....

■ Brainstorm the best work schedule or plan you think you'd be able to follow.

....

....

....

....

....

■ What obstacles test your creative mettle?

....

....

....

....

....

■ How do you shut out distractions and temptations?

....

....

....

■ Do you work long consecutive hours or function in energetic but erratic spurts?

....

....

....

■ Is the way you work compatible with your creative process?

....

....

....

■ Most creative people spend some time alone. Can you plan for some uninterrupted solitude?

....

....

....

■ A trigger that targets your desired behavior will help it become a habit. What powerful visual or sensory cue can you associate with the behavior you want to keep holy? The smell of coffee, or the click your metal door handle makes when you come back from walking the dog? What do you do without fail?

....

....

....

....

....

....

....

■ Some people use a ritual item to trigger falling into their creative routine. An amulet, particular music, a certain aroma. What works for you?

....

....

....

....

....

....

Picture This

If I can't picture it, I can't understand it.
–ALBERT EINSTEIN

To understand **A-P-P-L-E**, your brain has to first process the letters into a word, the word into a concept, and finally the concept into a context. But when you see a picture of an apple, you are immediately connected with the essence of *apple*, and can quickly make associations based on your personal experiences. The smell, the shiny red skin, the sound the first bite makes. A thought about forbidden fruit in the Garden of Eden. The New York City logo. The time your grandmother showed you how to remove the peel in one long spiral.

Pictures are a powerful and instinctual way to record, organize, and instantly convey a magnitude of meaning. And using them can super-size your capacity for associative thought and insight.

Single out a creative problem with which you're currently grappling. It can be a character's back-story, the structure of a song, how you'll arrange your living room, a work dilemma, the composition of an art piece, an organizational system you'd like to re-envision—anything.

Search online, in books, in magazines, in old photos, or elsewhere for imagery pertinent to your problem. Create a collection of relevant images. Do it digitally, tape your findings to the wall, make a collage of them, or put them in an album. Embellish them, connect them, and rearrange them. Share your work or keep it private. It's up to you.

Of all of our inventions for mass communication, pictures still speak the most universally understood language.
–WALT DISNEY

Sketch or jot down (or paste in) possibilities your visual exploration has brought up.

Visual Poetry

1. **Write a poem.** Or just photocopy some random text. A page from an instruction manual that came with your printer, an article about garden pests, even your tax bill.

2. **Cut it up.**

3. **Paste the pieces on the next page** in some way so that the visual form of the poem shapes the meaning of your words, the words convey something about the form of the poem, or both. Embellish further if you like.

Concrete or visual poems can be text simply printed in a way that forms a recognizable shape. Or they may involve sound, photography, and film. If you like the concept, explore it further.

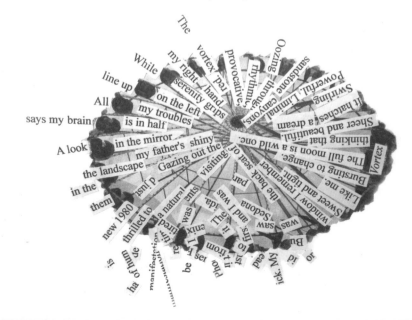

Heart

I think it's interesting that the word "heart" has the word "art" embedded in it. It also has the word "ear" embedded in it.
–JULIA CAMERON

Put Some Heart In Your Art. Love adds energy and depth to any creative project. Make it personal.

Invent a playful and personalized gift for someone you love. Remake a board game by covering the surfaces with pictures that represent personal addresses and favorite haunts. Craft a doll that looks like your favorite little girl or a handmade children's book. Decoupage a pencil cup with quotes from someone's favorite novel.

■ Who in your life might appreciate a highly personal gift, and what would you consider creating for them?

....

....

....

....

....

My favorite word is yearning because it suggests the deepest level of desire.

–ROBERT OLEN BUTLER

Take a cue from Robert Olen Butler. When you create a story, begin it with a sense of passion and longing.

If you get stuck in your writing, instead of trying to impress some anonymous audience, imagine your piece's impact on one specific reader. Write for that person.

Selling something? Whether it is your art, a DIY energy-saving windmill, or your revolutionary baby blanket, put yourself in the potential customer's shoes.

To create an evocative photograph, always look for a story. Try to imagine the emotional impact of what has happened or could happen before you snap your shutter. Look for motivation, desire, heart in everything.

■ Imagine an ideal reader, viewer, user, or listener. Who are they? What are they looking for when they open your book, visit your website, come to your opening, or press "play"?

....

....

....

....

■ What do you hope they get out of your work?

....

....

....

Specificity

Restrictions and limitations can work to your advantage.

Loss and limits can lead to great work. Shortages of time, materials, and even physical limitations can serve you creatively, especially for those creative people who suffer from having too many good ideas —all of them begging for attention.

Artist Janet Echelman would never have made her majestic interactive soft-net sculptures that light up in response to cell phone signals had she not arrived in Mahabalipuram, India, without her painting supplies and with no way to get more. In a hunt for alternative materials, she noticed local fishermen making nets and set out to see what she could do with the medium. One of her sculptures is shown below.

She Changes sculpture, Porto, Portugal. Photo: Madrugada Verde/Shutterstock.com

Take on one or more of the challenges below.

- *Work in an artistic medium you've never tried before. It could be mosaic, pipe cleaners, or food.*

- *Create a story in six words, like the famous "For sale, baby shoes, never worn."*

- *Write a limerick that begins, "There once was a _____ from _____ ..."*

- *Write a song in a genre you've never especially cared for.*

- *Draw or paint using only stark black and white. No shades of gray allowed.*

- *Limit yourself to only bold, sharp Anglo Saxon words (like ox and cow) in a poem. Consult Wikipedia's list of Anglo Saxon-derived words or use a print or online dictionary.*

- *If you're feeling ambitious, sign up for NaNoWriMo, along with about 200,000 other hopefuls, to write a 50,000-word novel in only 30 days.*

■ **Come back to this page afterward. How did it go?**

....

....

....

....

....

....

Our need will be the real creator.
–PLATO

Eliminate the Names

Capture more of what you observe and less of what you presume by describing things without using their names. It is a way to force a richer and more sensual narrative full of new words and analogies.

■ Hold an egg in your hand, or just imagine one. Feel the way its curve lies against your palm. Examine the texture. Is it cold? How does light bounce off its faint sheen? Fully describe that *thing*, without once using the word *egg* or any words associated with it (shell, yolk, etc.).

Now do the same for the nearest object to your right.

Think with Your Hands

Creativity is thinking up new things. Innovation is doing new things.
–THEODORE LEVITT

■ Tear off a sheet of aluminum foil. List five things you can make with it. (A bird? A hat?)

1 ....

2 ....

3 ....

4 ....

5 ....

■ Choose one and proceed. If you are unhappy with your first trial (or even if you aren't), start over with a fresh piece of foil. What did you discover the first time around that helped you with the second version?

....

....

....

....

Early Bird

God gives every bird his worm, but He does not throw it into the nest.
–P.D. JAMES

Are you an ingenious early bird or an innovative night owl?

Most people are better off doing their creative work in the morning, but there are late night geniuses too, and it seems to be a matter of genes and hormones more than choice. Stephen King and Toni Morrison's words flow best closer to dawn, but Bob Dylan and Michael Chabon work almost entirely at night.

■ When are you most creative?

....

....

■ And when, instead, are you most precise and accurate? Is there a time of day when you are better at difficult mental tasks?

....

....

It's a good idea to identify your creative prime time so you don't end up squandering it on other tasks. If you aren't sure, self-administer the Alternative Use Tests on the following pages. Do the first one when you get up in the morning, and the second before you go to bed at night. Don't peek ahead.

GOOD MORNING!

Give yourself five minutes to list as many alternative uses for a pencil as you can. Then fill at least one page with stream-of-consciousness writing about one of the ideas you produced. Don't look at the next page until bedtime.

GOOD EVENING!

Take five minutes to drum up as many alternative uses for a balloon as you can. Then fill at least one page with stream-of-consciousness writing about one of the ideas you produced.

Now compare. →

■ Did you come up with more suggestions in the morning or evening? Was your writing faster or more inventive by time of day?

....

....

■ Which list has the greatest variety?

....

....

■ Which list includes the most unusual and original ideas?

....

....

■ Was there enough difference to consider planning your time differently?

....

....

When you are too tired to work, a 15- to 30-minute nap can keep you going. But it is an art. You have to wake up before entering a deep sleep or you'll just be groggy. Thomas Edison, who was obsessed with maximizing his time, napped at his desk holding a metal ball over a tin plate so that he could wake himself right before fully drifting off. When the ball dropped, the clatter woke him.

Mental acuity and creativity do not keep the same hours. Experiment. The best time of day to write a short story may not be the best time of day to check for typos or edit. The time of day to dream up a new kind of business may not be the ideal hour to revise the budget.

See if crosswords, tangrams, online memory tests, or logic puzzles are easier for you before breakfast or after dinner.

■ Make a list of the tasks that require your alert and focused mind.

....

....

....

....

....

....

■ Make a list of the things that require inspiration and imagination.

....

....

....

....

....

....

■ Consider your lists, and note the time of day (if any) you are most likely to address each task. Is it consistent with when you are likely to do it best?

....

....

....

....

....

....

....

■ Can you change any part of your schedule to match what you do with the most efficient time to do it?

....

....

....

....

....

....

....

Mix It Up

Combinatory play seems to be the essential feature in productive thought.

—ALBERT EINSTEIN

Combinatory play is what Einstein called putting unrelated thoughts, topics, images, and ways of thinking together to generate new concepts.

Take it from Albert. Challenge yourself to find connections between randomly selected, unrelated words or pictures and surprise yourself with lots of unusual, quirky, and possibly splendid new ideas.

■ Play with the pictures on the next page and combine images to generate new ideas. For example: Put an alarm clock and a visor that shades the eyes from the sun together to create an alarm shade—a window shade that rises automatically to let the sun wake you at a preset time. Cross a vase and a book to get a weed vase—a garden dictionary with holes drilled in it to display dried twigs.

Draw lines connecting each object to another on the opposite side. Then, think of a way each pair could be combined. Be practical or fantastical as you please.

■ See what happens when you use six of the images on the previous page in a poem. Or pick any three to create a new literary character. Don't censor absurdity. Designer, artist, and photographer Karl Lagerfeld once said, "Absurdity and anti-absurdity are the two poles of creative energy."

Practice!
Practice!
Practice!

Is practice—experimentation and exercise with the goal of enhancing your skills—a part of your creative work? How so?

....

....

....

....

....

If so, how much time do you devote to it?

....

....

....

....

....

■ Does the hope of mastery in your chosen field affect your personal motivation? Does the rigorous practice required discourage or challenge you? Elaborate.

....

....

....

....

■ How important is it to you to be an expert at what you do? What level of competence are you hoping to reach?

....

....

....

....

■ How might you improve or add to your practice methods?

....

....

....

....

....

Old Photographs

Often poignant and mysterious, old photographs can make great creative prompts.

Where are these people headed? And why? What were they thinking when the photo was snapped? Tell about their world in words, in drawings, through a recipe, or on canvas.

Investigate an Ancestor

■ Search family albums, library collections, or online photo archives for an interesting-looking character. Take what you know and flesh out the rest. Give her a name if you don't know it. What music, ladies' fashion, or major world event featured in Aunt Gussie's hey-day? Use what you know and things you imagine to honor or spice up her memory. Include an image.

....

....

....

....

....

....

....

....

....

....

Music

Where words fail, music speaks.
—HANS CHRISTIAN ANDERSEN

Music is closely related to math in your neural circuitry, and they both seem to have a language all their own. Studying music can help you develop your associative thinking, pattern recognition, and feel for proportion and ratio. Some educators even say it could help you balance your checkbook.

Einstein loved the violin. Galileo was an accomplished flutist. And Steve Jobs knew how to play the guitar.

■ What role does music play in your life? What has it meant to you?

....

....

....

....

■ How does music affect you?

....

....

....

....

■ Do you write your own music? If not, have you ever tried?

....

....

....

....

Some suggestions if you don't have much music in your life, or even if you do:

- Learn to play a musical instrument—a harmonica if you need to travel light.

- Join a choral group or a church choir.

- Host a song fest or jam session. Invite friends who like singing to print out some lyrics and drop over with their guitars.

- Music as background noise can invigorate you or help you get into a creative zone. Experiment to see what works best for you.

- It may not be music to your ears, but there is some initial evidence that binaural (stereophonic) sound stimulates creativity. Numerous recordings are available online to sample. Some have background music and some consist of a droning noise that alternates from one ear to the other.

- Branch out. Set aside your favorite playlist and go far afield to shake up your neural circuitry. Listen with full attention to something you haven't heard before. French Rap? The Bulgarian State Television Female Vocal Choir? Already have eclectic taste? How about some Hoomii (Mongolian throat music) or the very haunting Tan Dun's *Water Passion* (after the passion of St. Matthew)?

Be Modern Art

Make a "self portrait."

1. Place your non-dominant hand in a loose fist at the bottom of this page. Hold a pen or pencil in your dominant hand.

2. Close your eyes and trace what feels like it would be the contour of your head and neck, using your fist as a guide.

3. Lift up your fist, but keep it hovering over the center of the page, to give you a sense of position.

4. Without opening your eyes, draw your face on the head you've created.

5. Open your eyes to see if you got a Picasso or a Jackson Pollock.

Don't stop there. That's hardly big enough to represent you and all you are. On this page, make a collage with a smattering of words, a caricature. Include a verbal selfie or an actual one, or a series of them. Move on to canvas or a large piece of wood. Be boldly who you are.

Don't Run On Empty

Pat yourself on the back for partial progress. Learn to accept compliments with a smile and a "thank you for noticing." You are on a creative journey and need to reward yourself along the way. Depriving yourself until you reach some distant goal is about as logical as withholding gas from your car until it gets from New York City to Los Angeles.

■ What praise and acknowledgment have you received recently?

....

....

....

....

....

....

....

....

■ What have you accomplished, big or small, monumental or incidental?

....

....

....

....

....

....

....

■ Make up a slogan or write your own lyrics to a familiar tune and hum it to yourself on the treadmill. And sing it loudly in your car alone.

....

....

....

....

....

....

....

Procrastination Is No Laughing Matter

Jerry Seinfeld thinks it's funny that he has been credited with this popular straightforward remedy for procrastination.

The idea is to cross out each day on a calendar only after you complete a specific daily task (a certain number of words, one hour, one song, or possibly a joke) to form a chain. After a while you just can't bear to break the chain and leave a bare space.

Conventional wisdom dictates that the shortest period of time it takes to begin a lasting habit is 30 days. So if you decide to give this method a whirl, stick with it for at least a month.

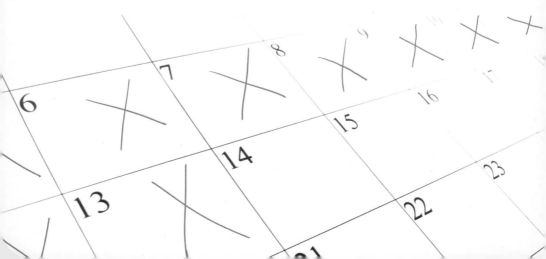

What is something you could accomplish on a daily basis toward your creative goal?

Dream Up Something

Now during my dream journey the following canon came into my head. ... But scarcely did I awake when away flew the canon, and I could not recall any part of it. On returning however, next day, in the same carriage...

–LUDWIG VAN BEETHOVEN

Dream language is symbolic, visual, sensory, and evocative. And its currency (alpha and theta brain waves) is the very stuff of creativity. Dreaming is one way your subconscious can show you what you already know. Or maybe something you don't.

Many geniuses—Salvador Dali, John Lennon, Kekulé, and Carl Jung, to name a few—asserted that dreams midwifed partially or even wholly formed work. It can be hard to reconcile the mystical with the objective when such gifts arrive effortlessly and seemingly out of the blue.

■ Do you remember your dreams? How often?

....

....

....

....

■ Are there any that stand out in your mind?

....

....

....

....

Take advantage of all those layered meanings, puns, and metaphors you come up with in your sleep by jotting down the first words you think of when you wake up. Dreams and dream residue can enhance your writing, comedy routine, interpretation of a song, or whatever you are trying to accomplish. Noting dreams often makes it easy to remember more of them. So will lying quietly for a few minutes before popping out of bed to start ticking off your to-do list.

Frankenstein's monster was Mary Shelley's literal nightmare. What images, words, colors, or sounds from one of your dreams might inspire a plot or character in your novel, a piece of artwork or music, a poem, or something else?

....

....

....

....

....

Dreams are a powerful form of consciousness.
–CAROLYN GREGOIRE

Creative Answers

The only questions that really matter are the ones you ask yourself.
–URSULA K. LE GUIN

To bring in more results, cast the widest net. But fish with the right bait.

How much you ask of yourself and others, and the way you ask, will determine how possible it is for you to create your best work and self—whether you intend to put your work on the map or just please yourself.

Start with the questions you ask yourself. Your brain is a problem-solving machine that will come up with an answer for anything you ask. But it will answer very literally. If you ask, "Why am I so dull, inept, and unproductive?" your brain will give you all the reasons why that might be the case. But if you ask, "How can I be more creative, be more efficient, or find a better way?" the list of possibilities your mind generates will be a call to action.

For that reason, *ask*. Don't simply tell yourself what you will do. If you vow to finish your chapbook, architectural plan, or business proposal by summer, your brain will accept that at face value. But if you ask yourself, "How can I finish that _____ (your choice)?" it will leap to find ways to do it.

■ What are some questions you can ask yourself?

....

....

....

■ How can you word them in the most empowering way?

....

■ Are you asking for what you really want? Have you taken the time to figure out what that is?

....

....

■ Who can you count on most for emotional support?

....

■ Who gives reliably insightful feedback?

....

■ Is there a teacher, an expert, or someone with a little time on their hands who can help you?

....

■ What people or institutions can lend, raise, or contribute money and other resources to further your projects?

....

ASK LOTS OF QUESTIONS. AND THEN ASK MORE.

Don't settle for the first "correct" answers. Life is not a standardized test.

Pose questions to yourself in the form of:

- *What if?*

- *Why not ____?*

- *How can ____?*

- *What would have happened if ____?*

Use the reply that Walt Disney insisted on among his staff: "Yes, if___?" (See page 10.)

Look for analogies and then ask yourself, "Can I ask my question in a different way?"

For a tailor-made support group, start a brainstorming/barn-raising group Barbara Sheer (*Wishcraft*)–style. Ask several friends to bring a goal, an obstacle, and someone you've never met to dinner for an evening of sharing resources and support. A typical group yields good ideas, connections, a system of accountability, and sometimes gifts and barters.

■ What five people do you think would be good group members?

1. ....

2.. ....

3. ....

4. ....

5. ....

■ What do you have to contribute, and what might you ask for in return?

....

....

....

....

....

....

....

....

....

....

Ask and you shall receive.
−MATTHEW 7:7-8

Mind Map

Mind map your idea to get the whole picture at a glance.

Tony Buzan popularized the use of visual diagrams in the 1970s as a way to think more creatively. He emphasized the positive impact color, images, and symbols have on our ability to process information and suggested the use of treelike branches radiating from the central topic.

There are many ways to use a mind map (look around online to explore the variety) and no way to get it wrong. Your map is a note to yourself. It can be brief or complex, rough-hewn or a work of art. In addition to saving thousands of words, pictures save time and stimulate tangential thoughts—often the seeds of creative fruit.

■ Turn the book sideways and, on the next page, create a mind map of an idea, anything from the seed of a novel to your thoughts on an issue that matters to you. Start by writing or sketching the main concept in the middle of the page. Map out major themes, connections, possible causes and effects, symbols—anything and everything important to your central idea.

Animal

Use words, music, paint, clay, blueprints, colored sand, Photoshop, or something else to create an imaginary animal. A prehistoric beast, futuristic pet, or mutant pest.

Apply what you know as you picture your creature. If you are a paleontologist, or just appreciate dinosaurs, you might want to discover a new species. If you sell cars, your pet might function as transportation. An exterminator or epidemiologist? How do you keep your creature from overpopulating?

■ Notes and ideas about the beast:

Sketches, images, or masterful rendering of the beast.

It's Physical

When my creative energy flowed most freely, my muscular activity was always greatest.

–NIETZSCHE

You maintain your creative tools. Writers back up computers, painters condition brushes, photographers clean cameras, and dancers replace worn-out ballet slippers.

But *you* are the one and only most important and irreplaceable piece of equipment in your creative arsenal. Your body is a precious commodity, and deserves the best care you're able to give it.

Exercise enhances your mood and measurably improves your ability to think, create, use good judgment, tolerate uncertainty, and take artistic risks. Haruki Murakami runs and swims. Joyce Carol Oates jogs. Sting does yoga.

■ What kind of exercise do you do to keep from getting rusty?

■ What about your sleep patterns and eating habits?

....

....

....

....

....

....

....

Studies that measure semantic memory, concentration, accuracy, and the ability to read facial expressions indicate that working through meals can make you more stressed and less creative.

■ Do you take a break for lunch? How do you spend that time?

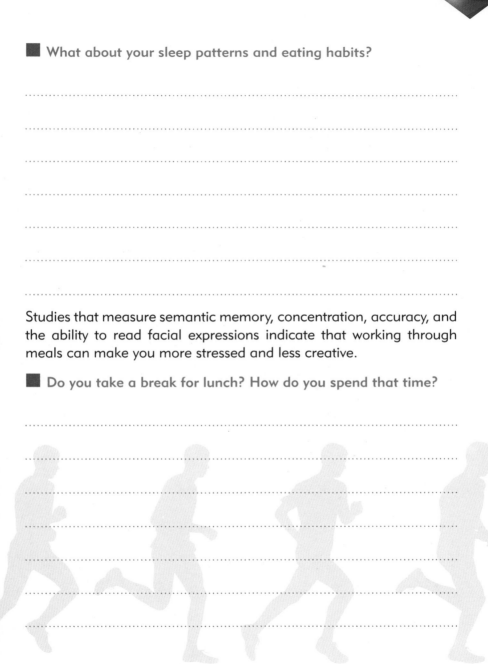

....

....

....

....

....

....

Be Bad

Or at least think about it.

When the pressure to produce good work is on, it can be hard to get started, get unstuck, or get perspective. Warm up by thinking of ways to make something terrible.

Pick one and go to town.

- Write a dreadful poem.
- Pair mismatched fabric samples and clashing paint chips to see just how gaudily you could redecorate your living room.
- Design a line of ludicrous pet accessories.
- Write a bad song or some terrible jokes to perform on open mic night.
- What laughable description can introduce the villain in your novel? How about opening with a ridiculous description of the weather?
- Make a list of all the ways you can bore your audience with a speech or kill a sales campaign.

■ What else do you want to do well that you could do badly first?

....

....

....

....

....

BAD IDEA SPACE

Working with Your Inner Critic

A man cannot be comfortable without his own approval.

—MARK TWAIN

A good inner critic knows what it is doing. It sees where your work isn't right, and insists that you do better because you can. If it tries to nit-pick too early in your process, it usually quiets down when reminded that minor errors are easily corrected and that it is important to with-hold judgment—because a crazy idea often leads to a brilliant result.

■ What does your inner critic do very well? How do you nurture that gift of acuity?

....

....

■ Is your critic ever a perfectionist? Impatient with your need to dabble with ideas?

....

■ What are some of the ways you keep it in place? For instance: Flirt with new ideas, sketch outlines and do first drafts in one location but do evaluations, edits, or touch-ups in another? Can you get up early to get your imagining done before your critic opens its beady eyes? (It is common for critical faculties to sleep in.)

....

Taming a Brutish Inner Critic

If your inner critic is incorrigible and apt to morph into a Mr. or Ms. Hyde, it can rip away your self-assurance, shut down your sense of play, and bring your flow down to a trickle just when you are poised to make a creative leap. Whether you are new at your craft or a seasoned pro, Hyde can sneak up to re-run old tapes of discouraging words, memories of failings, and lists of your real and imagined flaws. But you can stop listening.

■ What is your critic's *modus operandi?* When is it most likely to become unmanageable? Following a conversation with any particular person? When you're hungry, lonely, or exhausted?

....

....

....

....

....

■ How can you find ways to minimize or avoid precursors to inner critic run amok?

....

....

....

....

You can't erase hardwired thoughts, but you can derail them. Below are some common barbs. Use them as-is or amend them to reflect your critic's store of ammunition. (Who in your life said or implied any of these?)

Put a big red slash though each negative comment and replace it with an encouraging, positive statement. Include good marks, compliments, signs of progress, and what you just know to be true about yourself.

Just who do you think you are anyway? You're a fake.

....

....

That's weird. or *You're weird. People are going to laugh at you.*

....

....

Not interesting. Not good enough. (Dr. Seuss' first children's book was refused by at least 20 publishers.)

....

....

Your friend, sibling, or _____ *is way better than you.*

....

....

....

You failed at _____. *What makes you think can* _____ *now?* (Steven Spielberg was rejected three times by the prestigious USC film school.)

....

....

You got a poor grade in a class.

....

....

You don't have what it takes. You are too _____ *(old, young, dull, insufficiently educated, fat, shy, etc.).*

....

....

You're done. You only had (or have) one good book, painting, idea, or _____ *in you.*

....

....

What else?

....

....

....

....

Many people make up names for their inner pests to cut them down to size. Some favorites are Gremlin, Heckler, Monkey Mind, Nag, Perfectionist, Committee, and Judge. So take a deep breath and say something like:

"Yep, there's that old (substitute your pet name) _____! I know its tricks. If it doesn't have a useful suggestion then I'll just keep working."

■ What could you say to your critic the next time it wants to play rough?

....

....

....

....

....

■ In what ways could your inner critic be helpful, and how could you facilitate that?

....

....

....

....

....

....

■ Another common practice is to make or find an image that represents your personal needler. Do a preliminary sketch or paste an image in right here.

Have you decided to make it scary so you can confront its full power, or a little clownish to deflate it? Play with that image. Doodle on it. Put a band-aid on its lips. Or use a cartoon bubble to put new words in its mouth.

Forgive

What you resist persists.
–CARL JUNG

Forgiveness is powerful and healing. See if you can forgive some of your detractors.

■ Who has discouraged you?

....

....

....

....

■ Were they trying to help you in some misguided way?

....

....

....

....

....

■ What part of themselves may they have been trying to protect?

....

....

....

....

■ Can you forgive them?

....

....

....

....

■ Can you forgive yourself for not being perfect?

....

....

....

....

Art to Go

I like the ephemeral thing about theatre. Every performance is like a ghost—it's there and then it's gone.

–MAGGIE SMITH

Art with an expiration date has its charm. The ephemeral nature of live music and theater generates a type of suspense that can't be recorded. So do performance art and other art forms with a brief life span.

It can be very freeing to make something you don't mean to save or sell. Whether you decide to convey a particular message or just do it for the experience, it can unleash creative energy you didn't even know you had. Jot down or sketch some ideas:

What could you make out of materials meant... (Write or draw your responses.):

■ To dissolve? (wet sand on the beach, snow or ice, or wax?)

....

....

■ To topple? (blocks, stacks of stones?)

....

....

■ To wash away? (face or body paint, chalk on the sidewalk?)

. . . .

. . . .

■ To burn?

. . . .

. . . .

■ To fall like dominoes?

. . . .

. . . .

■ To be consumed?

. . . .

■ To blow away, rot, rust, rise into the air, be tossed away, or float down a river?

. . . .

. . . .

If you decide to photograph or videotape your momentary art, as does artist Andy Goldsworthy, your work could end up on coffee tables. That way you can have your cake and eat it too (literally, if you make something fabulous out of baked goods).

Or just do it again!

Physical Confidence

The mind is just another muscle.
—TED TURNER

Sometimes you can change how you feel inside by shifting your outside. Muscle up some confidence and creativity.

Your facial expression, your posture, the rhythm of your gait, and the oomph in your voice don't just announce who you are to the world. They also tell *you* who you are.

Charles, a composer who'd choked on an assignment, urgently needed a theme song for a new sitcom. Though nearly defeated, he was able to focus and quietly recall the way his breath had felt in his chest and the way his bare feet had swished against his carpet as he'd tapped out the rhythm while writing his first hit. After imitating his winning body language, he authored a new chorus and a bridge in less than an hour, much to his surprise.

Slump with your arms folded across your chest for a moment to see how stifling it feels. Then straighten your back, lower your shoulders, and drop your arms to your sides to gear up for some quicker thinking and playful creativity.

Think of a time you were at your best. What were you doing? How were you holding your body? Your head? Were you moving or still? What other physical sensations do you recall?

How Big Is Your Ask?

The art and science of asking questions is the source of all knowledge.
–THOMAS BERGER

■ How good are you at asking for what you need?

....

....

....

■ How often and under what circumstances do you ask for the support you need to pursue your creative goals?

....

....

....

■ What is it like for you to ask for emotional support?

....

....

....

■ For financial support?

....

....

....

■ For accurate and helpful feedback?

....

....

....

■ Do you ask for opportunities to show or share your stuff?

....

....

....

■ Are you getting what you need?

....

....

....

....

....

Forty Circles

Draw as many pictures in the circles below, one picture per circle, as you can in four minutes.

Working fast disinhibits you and makes it easier to get in the flow. Observe the number and types of responses you made under pressure without judgment.

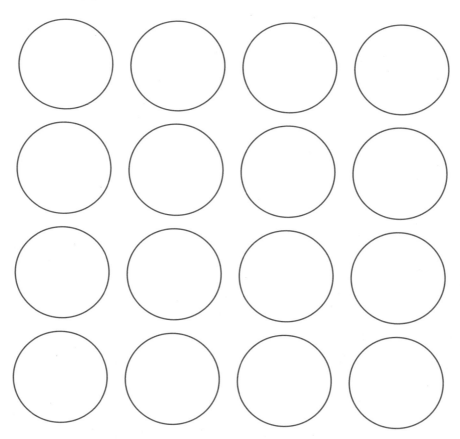

A version of this test was developed by Bob McKim, but popularized by Tim Brown's TEDTalk: Tales of Creativity and Play.

Sweet-Talking Your Inner Sloth

I like the word "indolence." It makes my laziness seem classy.
–BERN WILLIAMS

Sloth just wants to be safe and comfortable. Sloth tries to avoid risks and sweat.

Nearsighted, it favors small but certain pleasures at hand over attractive but distant rewards it can't see.

That's why, even though it knows very well that you are manipulating it, Sloth is easily plied. "As soon as we put in one more hour, we can sit down and have a latte and do a crossword" is all it takes. The rewards can be small as long as the wait is short. Make the goodies keep coming at reasonable intervals. (You don't want your sloth to turn into a glutton.) Eventually you will have formed a new work habit.

When the stakes are high, you might need to design a plan with some immediate negative consequence to make sure the sloth hops to. For example: Joe, a young father who had planned to get up 30 minutes early every morning to complete a special work assignment, just kept hitting the snooze button. Even though he was assured a promotion and a sizable raise once the job was done, Sloth had the upper hand. But when Joe set his alarm to go off only five minutes before a second alarm was set to go off in his three-year-old daughter's room, he woke easily and got to work.

■ When does your inner sloth tend to hold sway?

....

....

....

■ How do you manage your slothlike impulses?

....

....

....

■ What carrots and sticks are most effective at making your sloth cooperate?

....

....

....

■ What matters enough for you to sacrifice creature comforts in exchange for less certain rewards?

....

....

....

....

Pareidolia

If you look at any walls spotted with various stains or with a mixture of different kinds of stones, if you are about to invent some scene you will be able to see ... figures ... and strange expressions of faces, and outlandish costumes, and an infinite number of things which you can then reduce into separate and well conceived forms.

–LEONARDO DA VINCI

Take advantage of **pareidolia**, the psychological phenomenon that makes us see faces and animals in vague shapes like clouds or rocks, to come up with great pictures. Leonardo da Vinci did.

Whoops! A coffee spill. What can you make out of it? Draw what you see.

*Trace and embellish the forms
that jump out at you.*

The Creative Age

I feel that I am making daily progress.

–PABLO CASALS *(age 93, when asked why he continued to practice the cello three hours a day)*

Time spent cultivating a creative stance in life may be the best long-term investment you'll ever make.

The impulse to create art, music, poetry, and literature does not decline with age. And barring certain kinds of disabling illness, neither will your creative ability. As you get older, the experience and perspective you accumulate will lead you to new, rich, and fascinating expressions of your creativity. With a lifetime of stored data and fewer inhibitions, it can get easier to put things together in more novel and useful ways.

So if you don't retire your curiosity and keen interest in learning new things with the advent of whatever age bracket you currently find yourself in, you may just be headed toward the most creative time of your life.

Forget any notions you may have of milestones, deadlines for major accomplishments, or eventual rocking chairs on the porch. Whatever your age, now is the perfect time for tripod roller blades, learning a language, taking piano lessons, and learning *chisanbop* (Korean finger math).

■ How old are you now, and how would you describe your creative trajectory?

....

....

....

....

■ If you're not there yet, how do you envision life after 65?

....

....

....

....

■ What interests and activities do you expect to pursue over the long haul?

....

....

....

....

....

....

Doodle

A line is a dot that went for a walk.

–PAUL KLEE

Doodle here. Cross over this text and even onto the next page in any way that pleases you.

Go Big

Make something that is usually small into something big. For example, you could ...

- turn a tiny white lie into such a whopper it becomes a comedy routine.
- use a grid or a projector to enlarge a baby picture. Make it billboard size to paste on a nursery wall or in the garage to welcome you home.
- make a very many layered birthday cake.

What would you like to do in a big way? How could you accomplish it? Describe and draw your thoughts.

Does Your Work Have Legs?

Start collecting ideas about how to send your work out into the universe.

Circle any that apply to you:

- Submit articles to journals and other publications.
- Sign up for a class where your work will be seen and critiqued by others.
- Volunteer to read or present at your public library or at a Rotary Club.
- Join a writers' group, artists' group, band, or other special interest club.
- Submit a book proposal.
- Self-publish.
- Invite friends to see your work.
- Find galleries or restaurants that will display your art.
- Enter contests.
- Put something up for sale online.
- Write an article for a professional journal.
- Start a blog.
- Write book reviews online.
- Create a website for your work.
- Check out local theater groups to see if they need actors, writers, musicians, or scenery painters.
- Search the internet for both local and worldwide contacts.

■ For each circled item, what have you done and what was the result? If you haven't done it yet, make a specific commitment here, complete with target date.

....

....

....

....

....

....

....

■ What else have you tried or thought about doing?

....

....

....

■ If you haven't started yet, what's holding you back? When do you think you will be ready?

....

....

....

....

Work with Your Muse

Who knows where inspiration comes from.
Perhaps it arises from desperation.
Perhaps it comes from the flukes of the universe,
the kindness of the muses.

−AMY TAN

Choose a muse and ask for help.

Once upon an ancient time, artists and poets dedicated major works to their muses. They made offerings of honey and fruit, prayed, and begged for assistance. It was an arrangement. A muse, or daemon, shouldered the responsibility for inspiration, and the artist's job was to work hard.

Your brain is a small universe. Vastly complex, it has 86 billion neurons, and perhaps as many as 100 trillion connections between those neurons. There are more connections in your brain than all the stars in the Milky Way, more neurons than there are galaxies known to man. Creativity is like quicksilver and we only understand a thimbleful of what there is to know about it.

Most of the time, genius grows out of an alternating pattern of analytical thinking and subconscious activity, but occasionally it arrives fully formed (as a song, a blueprint, or a poem). The elusive spark seems forever poised somewhere between magic and science. We can sense it, fan it, watch it light up the medial prefrontal cortex on an MRI, nurture it and marvel at the results, but never pin it down.

Whether divine intervention is real or not, suspending disbelief can be a psychological edge. Prayers, rituals, and trinkets are proven to provide a sense of control, and improve performance. Confiding to a muse in your journal or in an imaginary conversation can order your thoughts, be cathartic, and who knows? Maybe someone is listening.

■ Do you believe in divine inspiration? Do you feel you have a "muse"? Human or otherwise?

....

....

....

....

....

■ Whether envisioning your muse as a character, as a part of your-self, or as your higher being, what would you want it to do for you?

....

....

....

....

....

What If?

In the beginner's mind there are many possibilities,
in the expert's mind there are few.
–SHUNRYU SUZUKI

What if it were possible...?

■ Push your daydream envelope. Make a list of at least **30 things** that would thrill you to the very bone if they ever became a reality. Include every ambition, travel idea, hope about a relationship, accomplishment at work, and more. Sit down alone or with a friend to daydream on paper. Then turn the page.

1. ....

2. ....

3. ....

4. ....

5. ....

6. ....

7. ....

8. ....

9. ....

10. ....

11. ....

12. ....

13. ....

14. ....

15. ....

16. ....

17. ....

18. ....

19. ....

20. ....

21. ....

22. ....

23. ....

24. ....

25. ....

26. ....

27. ....

28. ....

29. ....

30. ....

■ Now, go back and bring into play the "Yes, if..." strategy from page 10, to turn possibilities into plausibilities.